W9-BAL-681

"Are you tired? Worn out? Burned out on religion?
Come to me. Get away with me and you'll recover your
life. I'll show you how to take a real rest. Walk with me
and work with me—watch how I do it. Learn the
unforced rhythms of grace. I won't lay anything heavy
or ill-fitting on you. Keep company with me and you'll
learn to live freely and lightly."

Matthew 11:29-30 (MSG)

201 GREAT QUESTIONS

TO HELP SIMPLIFY YOUR LIFE

JERRY D. JONES

NavPress
BRINGING TRUTH TO LIFE
P.O. Box 35001, Colorado Springs, Colorado 80935

The Navigators is an international Christian organization. Our mission is to reach, disciple, and equip people to know Christ and to make Him known through successive generations. We envision multitudes of diverse people in the United States and every other nation who have a passionate love for Christ, live a lifestyle of sharing Christ's love, and multiply spiritual laborers among those without Christ.

NavPress is the publishing ministry of The Navigators. NavPress publications help believers learn biblical truth and apply what they learn to their lives and ministries. Our mission is to stimulate spiritual formation among our readers.

The people quoted in this book each have profound and thoughtful words worthy of our consideration. However, using their quotes for the purposes of this book in no way implies that we necessarily endorse or agree with all of their beliefs or values.

© 1999 by Jerry Jones
All rights reserved. No part of this publication may be reproduced in any form without written permission from NavPress, P.O. Box 35001, Colorado Springs, CO 80935
www.navpress.com
ISBN 1-57683-146-9

Scripture quotations marked (NLT) are taken from the *Holy Bible, New Living Translation*, ©1996. Used by permission of Tyndale House Publishers, Inc., Wheaton, Ilinois 60189. All rights reserved; *The Message: New Testament with Psalms and Proverbs* by Eugene H. Petrson, ©1993, 1994, 1995, used by permission of NavPress Publishing Group, and *The New Jerusalem Bible* (NJB), copyright © 1985 by Darton, Longman & Todd, Ltd., and Doubleday & Company, Inc.

Printed in the United States of America

1 2 3 4 5 6 7 8 9 10 11 12 13 14 15 / 05 04 03 02 01 00 99

FOR A FREE CATALOG OF
NAVPRESS BOOKS & BIBLE STUDIES,
CALL 1-800-366-7788 (USA)
OR 1-416-499-4615 (CANADA)

Contents

INTRODUCTION FOR "201 GREAT QUESTIONS TO HELP SIMPLIFY YOUR LIFE"

Is this book for you?
It is if your search is for:

Less
- of the rat race
- clutter and pressure
- stress
- noise and complication

More
- peace and quiet
- satisfaction and fulfillment
- clarity and purpose
- time for the people and things you hold most dear
- joy and freedom
- simple pleasures
- focus on significance to God, to living a life worth living

The Power of the Question

This book is designed to help you find what you are searching for, to help you live a more simple life. But this is not a book of answers. It is a tool box full of ready-to-use questions to share with one or more friends and loved ones who are on a similar journey. As author and Theologian Sam Keen says, "nothing shapes our lives so much as the questions we ask."

Does living a more simple life equal joy, happiness, satisfaction, fulfillment, peace, contentment, and a deeper richer life? Not in and of itself. In fact, none of these are possible unless we seek *first* the kingdom of God "and make it our primary concern" (Mt. 6:33 NLT). As a wise man once reminded us, "God made man simple; man's complex problems are of his own devising" (Eccles. 7:29, Jerusalem Bible). But in seeking God's kingdom, our priorities are changed. We become less caught up in all the complexities and rabbit trails of this world and are able to live the more simple, contented life that is at the core of our deepest yearnings.

So what are the questions at the heart of your search for simplicity? As author Gregg LeVoy reminds us, "We must come bearing questions. . . . without [them] there is no discovery."

Use this book within the context and safety of people you know and love to help you rediscover those things that are most important to you, to help you make more sense out of your life. To help you, as John Michael Talbot writes, become less "preoccupied with the superficial at the expense of the meaningful."

A FEW SUGGESTED GUIDELINES AS YOU USE THIS BOOK

These questions are intended to be used as:

- Conversation starters to guide your search for a more simple, intentional, purpose-centered life.
- A way to discuss and, in so doing, better formulate in your own heart and mind the pathway to spiritual and personal health.
- A way to get to know yourself—and others—better as you discuss your questions, feelings, longings and beliefs together.
- A springboard for experiencing the joy of soul-sharing with trusted friends both old and new—those who will join in the question-asking, listen, and help bring another perspective.
- Discussions starters to help you gain a better understanding of how God fits into the big picture of your life.
- A way to encourage and stimulate serendipitous discovery and the healing qualities of connecting with others in the context of community.
- A (mostly) non-threatening, relaxed way to build bridges with those you love and care about.

There is no need to be frightened on this marvelous discovery journey.

The questions have been divided into three categories, progressing from lighter questions to those that require a greater degree of mutual trust, safety and understanding. Proceed at you own comfort level.

Some suggested places to use this book:
- In the living room or around the dinner table.
- While traveling with friends or family. (One handy place to keep this book would be in the glove box of your automobile.)
- During the opening minutes of your small group discussion, Bible study, or Sunday school class to help members share and get better acquainted.
- With your mate while setting priorities as you dream and plan your future together.
- On a date.
- With a counselor.
- Over a cup of coffee with a good friend.

Our hope is that this book will encourage and challenge you toward a new, fresh perspective on the meaning of life among those you know and trust—and who desire the best for you. It is only in the sharing of who we are that we can live a life worth living.

Note: When using these questions in the context of a small group, determine the ground rules that will guide your sharing and discussion. Here are some suggested guidelines for your consideration:

- **Confidentiality:** I will not share with anyone outside the group the personal things that are shared by those in the group.
- **Honesty:** I will be forthright and truthful in what is said. If I do not feel I can share something, I will say, "I pass" for that question.
- **Openness:** I will be candid with others in appropriate ways and allow others to share for themselves.

- **Respect**: I will not judge others, give advice, or criticize.
- **Care**: I will be open to the needs of others in appropriate ways.

(Adapted from "Spiritual Autobiography" by Dick Peace, NavPress, pg. 19)

1

Imagine that you are going to live on a ranch one hundred miles from the nearest store. How will that change your lifestyle? What might you lose and what might you gain?

2

If you were to move into a thirty-six-foot sailboat and sail around the world for two years, what would you take with you?

3

What does "simplicity" mean to you?

4

How are "getting better organized" and "living a life of simplicity" different? How are they the same?

5

Sam Walton, billionaire founder of Wal Mart, was often seen riding around Bentonville, Arkansas, in his old Ford pickup. What does this say about him? Name one item you use regularly even though you could afford a more expensive model.

6

When you experience exhaustion, does it usually take the form of physical or mental weariness? What three circumstances in your life contibute to this? Do you have any control over these things?

7

How would it impact your lifestyle if you earned three times as much money as you do now? What relationship exists between your income and the simplicity of your lifestyle?

8

If you had been God's chief engineer during creation, in what ways would you have altered the design of the human body for greater simplicity of function?

9

Which is most simple to you:
a circle, a square, or a triangle?
Why? What does this say to you
about your understanding
of simplicity?

10

If you were to establish a rule in your house that anything that was not used at least once a month would be tossed or given away, how would that simplify or complicate your life?

11

When does your telephone become more of a nuisance and less of a convenience? What changes can you make in your telephone habits to simplify your life?

12

When you reflect on where your life is headed, would you say that you are more in flight or in quest? How does the simple life play into that?

13

Think back to your grandparents or great-grandparents. In what ways did they live a more complicated life or a more simple life than you do?

14

What are three things that drive people to lead unnecessarily complicated lives?

15

If living a simple life is as healthy and satisfying as many believe, why do so few people choose to do it?

16

What are the simple pleasures you most relish (for example, napping in a hammock or picnicking in a scenic spot)? How do such experiences feed your soul?

17

Do you get any newspapers or magazines that you seldom read? If so, name them. Why do you continue to subscribe?

18

In what ways, if any, are you sacrificing quality of life (more joy) in order to achieve a higher standard of living (more stuff)?

19

It has been said that "one person's simplicity is another's complexity." How might this be true of you and a close friend or your spouse?

20

If you were to pare your life down to the essentials, what five things would you keep and what ten things would you let go of?

21

Do you know anyone who has made the decision not to have a TV in their home? If so, what were their reasons? How might the absence of a TV in your home help simplify your life?

22

If you had a personal staff of five people — including a live-in maid, a full-time gardener, and a full-time cook — how could they help you live a life of simplicity? Are there ways in which they would complicate your life? What part of your life would they *not* be able to help you simplify?

23

Due to a financial setback, you have been forced to cut your personal consumption of goods in half for the next seven years. What will you choose to eliminate? What will you miss most, and what might you gain in the process?

24

Does living a simplified life impact the enviornment in any meaningful way? Explain.

25

Do you believe the yearning for a simpler way of life has been with humankind since the beginning, or is it relatively recent? Explain.

26

Since the 1950s, our houses have doubled in size, on average, while at the same time our family size has been cut in half. Why do you think that is? How does this help or hurt our efforts to live more simply?

27

How would it impact your lifestyle if you did not have a car? What would you stop doing that you do now out of habit?

28

What are some things you tend to do in pairs (such as driving and talking on the phone, or conversing with someone while watching TV)? Does this doubling up add more complexity to your life or reduce it?

29

Which room in your house do you most enjoy spending time in? What steps could you take that would allow you to spend more time in this room?

30

How many loads of laundry does each person in your household produce each week? What might you do to reduce that number?

31

In your opinion, is it easier to live a life of simplicity in the country, in a small town, in a suburb, or in a city? Why?

32

Change seldom happens without first asking questions. What are three questions you have about living a life of greater simplicity?

33

What can we learn from children about simplicity?

34

Would you say that a desire to live a simpler life is common in our society? What evidence do you see to support your opinion?

35

In what ways might complexity be considered a necessary aspect of our culture? Is complexity increasing or decreasing? How?

36

What is the difference between a livelihood and a life?

37

In what ways, if any, might living a life of simplicity become irresponsible?

38

If the world were to shrink overnight and everyone was forced to live in one-quarter of the space they currently occupy, how would you cope?

39

When preparing for a trip, do you pack only what you will need? Or do you also pack many of the things you *might* need? Why?

40

Does simplicity reduce or increase one's enjoyment of life? If so, how? If not, why not?

41

During what period of your life
was your lifestyle the simplest?
What made it so? How happy
were you then?

42

In your opinion, does simplicity
require that you impoverish
yourself? Why or why not?

According to author Elaine St. James, "There is so little we really need and you can always get along without it." What are three material things that you believe you really need, and how would your life be different if you were forced to function without them?

44

Does living a life of simplicity require that you be less dependent on others or more dependent? In what ways?

45

Do you need faith to live a life of simplicity? If so, faith in what?

46

What does it mean to find the sacred in the ordinary? In what ways have you done this?

47

What "toys" in your life tend to complicate more than simplify? How?

48

In what ways is choosing to lead a simplified life like a spiritual conversion?

49

In the 1840s Henry David Thoreau lived for two years in a small cabin near Massachusetts's Walden Pond, where he focused on "the essential facts of life." Can you see yourself ever doing something like that? Why or why not?

50

The Bible speaks often of moderation. What does moderation look like in a society of abundance? In what ways would moderation help simplify your life?

51

Is it selfish to want to simplify your life? Why or why not?

52

Nearly everyone has heard the slogan "bigger is better." What are three examples of where this slogan might be true? What are three examples of where it might be false?

53

In the Lord's Prayer, the only material thing asked for is bread, a necessity of life. What conclusions, if any, should we draw from that?

54

Have you ever regreted
volunteering for something that
significantly complicated your
life? If so, would you do it again?
Why or why not?

55

If you were to "drop out of the rat race" and do something you have dreamed of doing for years, what would you do?

56

What is the relationship between
simplicity and freedom?

57

What are the differences between
activity and productivity? When
are you most likely to mistake
one for the other in your
personal life?

58

What role do others expectations play in your daily or weekly schedule? Are you comfortable with the proportion of your resources currently devoted to servicing the requests or demands of other?

59

If you were to hire your best
friend or mate as a consultant to
streamline your life, what advice
do you think that person
would give?

60

Imagine for a minute
that we have just experienced
a worldwide calamity and all
normal food distribution channels
have ceased to function—
no grocery stores, convenience
stores, or restaurants.
This calamity will last for
ten years. What will you do
to survive? Will your life be
complicated or simplified by this?

61

Read the words of Jesus printed on page 1. In what ways do Jesus' words depict your practice of the faith? In what ways is your experience different?

62

For you, what would be the hardest part about living simply?

63

Let's say you are given the opportunity to trade any one thing in your life for something else. How will you complete this sentence: "I would like to trade _____ in my life for _____."

64

Where do you need to be more ruthless with the clutter in your life?

65

If you were to sell half of what you own, in what ways would you be deprived?

66

Who are the "Joneses" in your life you are trying to keep up with? Why are you doing it?

67

Someone once said, "we often become preoccupied with the superficial at the expense of the meaningful." What are these superficial things in your life? What are meaningful things you may be overlooking?

68

Are you living mostly in the past, in the present, or in the future? Would it simplify your life if you were to live more fully in the present? If so, how could you do that?

69

Of all the changes you would
need to make to simplify your
lifestyle, which one would require
the most courage? Why?

70

Henry David Thoreau once wrote,
"That man is the richest whose
pleasures are the cheapest."
Do you agree or disagree? In what
way is this true or not true
in your own life?

71

What is your idea of success in life? How simple or complex would your life have to be for you to achieve that success?

72

If you were to give your life a spring cleaning, where would you begin?

73

Complicated machines are more likely to break down than are basic tools. Is your weekly schedule more like a complicated machine or a simple tool? In what ways, if any, do you wish it were different?

74

If you were to choose to live "close to the earth," what would that look like for you?

75

Thinking back over the past month, what have you bought because of an ad that you would not have bought otherwise? How do you feel about the purchase now?

76

Is it primarily internal or external influences that cause us to lead complicated lives? Explain.

77

What are the things you most value in life but do not have enough of?

78

Describe a time when you stopped and asked yourself, *Why am I living my life this way?* What brought you to that point? What changes did you make, if any? What has been the result?

79

Imagine that God has decided to do an intercontinental swap. He's going to pluck a family from an Asian village and move them into your house. Simultaneously, He's going to place you and your family in the other family's home—a two-room bamboo hut (no running water, dirt floor, no motor transportation). In this swap, who gains what and who loses what?

80

In what ways might fasting help teach the difference between wants and needs? What other disciplines or experiences could teach the same thing?

81

Does generosity go hand in hand with living a life of simplicity? Why or why not?

82

If you were to get serious about
living a simple lifestyle, who in
your circle would encourage you?
Who would discourage you?
What would their reasons be?

83

Many investment counselors recommend that you diversify your investments to protect them. On the other hand, some of the most successful investors risk all their resources on one or two investments they really believe in. Considering that your life is your greatest investment, which investment strategy are you following? How and why?

84

Do you seek simplicity primarily for practical reasons (to be better organized, less hectic, more economical, et cetera) or to replenish your soul? Why? Is it possible to have one outcome without the other?

85

What is the highest-maintenance part of your life right now? What would it take to make it low-maintenance?

86

If your doctor told you that you had only six months to live, what would be most important to you? How would you change your priorities, schedule, habits, et cetera?

87

Name three things in your life that require more time or energy than they are worth. What can you do to simplify or eliminate those things?

88

Is it possible to have simplicity without frugality? Explain.

89

How many credit cards do you have? In an average month, what is the total of their balances? How do your credit cards help or hinder you in your pursuit of the simple life?

90

Some believe the best way to leave this world is how you came in—with not a dime to your name. Do you agree or disagree with this "die broke" philosophy? Why? In what ways might this philosophy help you live a simpler life?

91

Would winning the lottery make your life more simple or more complex? How?

92

Some people never purchase new things without getting rid of a corresponding number of things they already own. What would be the advantages and disadvantages of having a "no accumulation" rule for your life? How could you make it work?

93

Who among your friends and acquaintances have made a conscious decision to have less stuff in their life? How did they do it and why?

94

If you were to budget your time like you budget your money, where would you budget more time? Where would you budget less time?

95

When are you most likely to buy something you don't need, won't use, or can't afford?

96

Is it possible to live a life of simplicity without having a good deal of restraint? Explain. What is the most difficult part about learning restraint?

97

If your goal was to learn restraint and moderation over the next four months, how would you set about doing it? How would you teach them to children?

98

What is "enough"? How can we know when we have it?

99

Is well-being equal to an increasing net worth? If so, in what ways? If not, why not?

100

What is at the root of our desire for more?

101

What do you think Robert Browning meant when he said, "Less is more"? How or when has that been true in your own life?

102

It is not only the bad things in our lives that we need to let go of to live a simpler life; sometimes even good things clutter our lives. What are four good things you need to let go of?

103

When you buy more of something (a bigger house, more clothes, a fancier car), what are at least three things you have to give up in exchange?

104

If you were to move to a place where no one knows who you are, would it be easier or harder to live a life of simplicity? Why?

105

If God offered you perfect peace and happiness as long as you agreed to give up all your wealth and your status in the community, would you accept the offer? Why or why not?

106

Have you ever spent so much time working to buy things that you had no time left over to enjoy those things? If so, what have you learned from that experience?

107

What do you think Thomas à Kempis meant when he said, "Blissful are the simple, for they shall have much peace." What relationship exists between simplicity and peace? Is it possible to have one exist without the other? Explain.

108

Why is it considered unacceptable in our society to wear the same skirt or shirt several times during the same week? If you did it anyway, how might that simplify your life?

109

We live in a land of plenty,
yet we often have a nagging sense
of discontentment. What is the
antidote to discontentment?

110

Do you have any consistent
ceremony, liturgy, or ritual in
your life? If you do, how might
that help you in living a life
of simplicity?

111

John Michael Talbot writes, "There's nothing magical about solitude that makes God suddenly appear. God is everywhere all the time. It's just that most of the time we are so busy with everything else that we don't notice." How does time alone with God help you better understand the purpose and priorities for your life?

112

Cornelius Plantinga, Jr.,
once said, "A loss of silence is as
serious as a loss of memory and
just as disorienting." How has the
"loss of silence" been disorienting
in your life? What are the steps
you have taken (or can take) to
regain some silence?

113

Do you have a tendency to run from silence? Why or why not?

114

What is the closest thing you have to a personal sanctuary— a place where you can be alone for thinking, dreaming, praying? What has the solitude and stillness you've found there meant to you?

115

What family traditions could enable you to enjoy the holidays while avoiding commercial pressures to consume excessively?

116

In what ways do you practice moderation in your diet?

117

In what ways does trying to keep a house immaculate complicate a person's life?

118

Describe a time when you went to visit someone whom you considered to be living "below their means." What was it that most surprised you about their home? Their lifestyle?

119

What items are you most likely to buy in bulk? How might buying in bulk help simplify your life?

120

Think about your kitchen for a moment. If you were to keep only those knives you really need, how many would you keep? Ask yourself the same question concerning your pots and pans.

121

In many parts of the world, homes have no closets or other places to store stuff, except for maybe a few hooks on the wall. How would you function without closets? What could we learn from those who have no need for closets?

122

How might living a simple life
enable us to:
► play more with our children?
  ► care more for our elders?
    ► plant more beautiful
      flowers and trees?
    ► read more books?
  ► make more music or
    paint some pictures?
► spend more time doing things
  that grow the soul?

123

When thinking about living the simple life, what part of you feels this makes no sense, and what part of you feels that your life will make no sense without it?

124

Václav Havel, president of the Czech Republic, once said, "Hope is not the conviction that something will turn out well, but the certainty that something makes sense, regardless of how it turns out." In what ways do you believe that living a life of simplicity makes sense, regardless of how it turns out?

125

In many cultures around the world it is a custom to take your shoes off at the front door, using only socks, slippers, or bare feet inside the house. How might adopting such a custom help us simplify our lives?

126

How does the choice of floor covering in your home impact simplicity in your life?

127

How might having no yard
(or a very low-maintenance yard)
help simplify your life? Is this
something you would consider?
Why or why not?

128

Are the demands of your current job compatible with living a simpler life? Why or why not?

129

According to author Christopher Lasch, advertising causes consumers to be "perpetually unsatisfied, restless, anxious, and bored." If true, how does this make life more complex? How does advertising create dissatisfaction in your life?

130

If you could invent a machine that would greatly reduce the complexity of life, what would it do?

131

When it comes to living a life of simplicity, where do your head and your heart most disagree? Where do they most agree? What would be an acceptable compromise?

132

The Internet, satellite television, and other technologies are expressions of the belief that more information is better. How has having access to more information made your life more complex or more simple?

133

Francis of Assisi believed that simplicity is an antidote to our constant hunger for more and more. Do you agree or disagree? How might it work as an antidote?

134

Elizabeth Seton once wrote,
"The gate of Heaven is very low;
only the humble can enter it."
Does simplicity require humility?

135

How do holidays complicate your
life? What could you do to make
them more simple?

136

What are the differences between simplifying your life and trying to escape your responsibilities?

137

Simone Weil once wrote, "Grace fills empty spaces, but it can only enter where there is a void to receive it." What are you willing to empty from your life to make more room for grace?

138

If you could take any kind of personal retreat, where would you go, how long would you stay, and what would you hope to discover about how you are currently living your life?

139

What are your greatest fears and insecurities about living a life of simplicity?

140

When making purchases, do you tend to buy fewer things that are more expensive or more things that are less expensive? Why? What are the advantages of one approach over the other?

141

It has been said that progress
comes from daring, not adapting.
In your search for simplicity,
where do you need to be
more daring?

142

Do you have a "Sabbath day" in your week? In what ways do you protect this day as a time set aside for family, personal, and spiritual nourishment?

143

How does telling the truth simplify or complicate your life?

144

In what ways was Jesus' life
a simple one? What can we learn
from His example?

145

Imagine for a moment that Jesus
is living in a family similar to
yours (same number of family
members) somewhere in your
community. How might His
lifestyle differ from the
one you lead?

146

As professional speaker Rosie Perez says, "The refrain goes, 'It's one for the money, two for the show, three to get ready, three to get ready, three to get ready . . .' " What is the "perfect moment" that you are waiting for to make the life changes you desire?

147

When did your life begin to really get complicated? Why?

148

If you viewed your life as a long journey, what is the excess baggage—traditions, possessions, beliefs, affections, motivations— that is most burdensome in keeping you from enjoying your trip?

149

If living a life of simplicity
represents your Garden of Eden,
what represents the forbidden
fruit for you? Why?

150

In our hectic, materialistic society, people living a simple life are looked at as nonconformists. How do you feel about being looked at in that way?

151

Winston Churchill once said,
"All great things are simple, and
many can be expressed in a single
word: freedom; justice; honor;
duty; mercy; hope." How would
you express the "great things"
in your life?

152

There are many outer, visible things one must do to begin living a life of simplicity. But what are the inner, invisible requirements?

153

What is your first priority:
to simplify your work life or to
simplify your personal life?
In your case, is it possible to do
one without the other?

154

Some schoolchildren wear
uniforms to school. How would
you feel if the adults in your
workplace had to wear uniforms
too? How might it help
simplify your life?

155

What are some of the things that a busy life leaves no time for?

156

What are those things you feel most obligated to? Why? When does your sense of obligation lead to unnecessary clutter in your life?

157

If you were to stop doing
one of these things you've always
done simply because you felt you
should, what would you
stop doing?

158

Do you tend to live your life
around things that are truly
important or around things that
are merely urgent? Explain.

159

What changes would be required in your primary relationships in order for you to simplify your life?

160

In what areas do you feel least in charge of your life? Why? How could simplicity help put you back in charge?

161

In general, does technology complicate or simplify your life? How?

162

What is the difference between simplicity and poverty? Between simple and spartan?

163

Do you have a budget? Do you live within it? In what ways can living on a budget help you experience the kind of life you most desire?

164

How do you distinguish between your wants and your needs? If you were counseling a child or a friend, how would you help that person tell the difference?

165

In what ways does spending
bring fulfillment? Is it more likely
to relieve stress or add to it?
Explain.

166

Do you believe that the best
things in life are free?
Why or why not?

167

If you were to lose all your possessions in a fire, which items would you be least likely to bother replacing? Why? What's keeping you from getting rid of those things now?

168

Consider an era in the past when you would have been required to grow your own food, make your own clothes, and build your own shelter. If things were still the same today, what would you most like about this life? What would you least like?

169

What kinds of pets have you had in your lifetime? How did they complicate or simplify your life?

170

Think of the items you routinely throw in the trash. What lifestyle changes would enable you to cut this material in half?

171

A "pack rat" is someone who keeps lots of things around, regardless of whether he or she has any need for them. Think for a minute about yourself and your best friend or spouse. Of the two of you, who is most like a "pack rat"? In what ways?

172

If you were to live a more childlike life, how would your life be less complicated or more complicated?

173

A. W. Tozer once wrote, "Contentment with earthly goods is the mark of a saint." In what ways are you content with your earthly goods?

174

How important is play in living a life of simplicity?

175

What did Gandhi mean when he said, "Live simply so that others may simply live"? How have you seen this statement to be true or false?

176

In what ways can living a simple life unburden the soul?

177

When choosing to live a life of simplicity, what five things must you say yes to? What five things must you say no to?

178

If you were coaching a child
about how to live a simpler life,
what personal experiences of
your own would you bring up?

179

Pretend that today you have decided to make some radical changes that will move you toward a life of simplicity. Based on this turning-point decision, describe your life as it will be five years from now.

180

Some say it is impossible to be happy until we know what we love. What do you most love? How could you reorganize your life so that you could give more attention to what you love?

181

If you were to simplify your life by being faithful to only a few deep concerns, what would be three of those concerns?

182

Do you ever feel that your life is like a stock portfolio—that you are investing in a wide variety of things, hoping that at least one of them will come up a winner? Explain. What keeps you from being more focused or purpose-driven?

184

Are you living a d
Why or why no
would you
de

183

Many species of [...]
pruned on a r[...]
remain produ[...]
were a tr[...]
commitme[...]
would yo[...]
for [...]

185

Writer Helen Nearing once wrote, "All is . . . fleeting. Will one be there to hear and see tomorrow? If not, let's taste it deeply now, take it into our being, chew and absorb it." At this point in your life, what is it you'd most like to taste deeply, to absorb?

186

Adventurer Elsa Buchner once said, "Security is certainly wonderful to have, but not at the price of inertia. I'll have plenty of that in the grave." In what ways might your desire for security win the tug-of-war over your desire to simplify your life?

187

Do you consider your life and affections to be highly focused or widely scattered? In what ways? How might you become more focused than you are now?

188

What in your past do you need to confront to help you in the letting go? How can confrontation— being brutally honest with yourself and others—help you move toward a life of simplicity?

189

It has been said that true joy and real greatness came from striving downward. Do you agree or disagree? In what ways are you "striving downward"?

190

Many believe that the secret to happiness is not in getting more but in wanting less. Is your tendency to be focused more on the "getting more" or on the "wanting less"? In what ways?

191

Do you have many times when you feel as if you're not getting anything important done? Give an example. What can you do to place more emphasis on those things that matter most?

<u>192</u>

Obituaries usually focus on outward accomplishments and seldom on such things as spending quality time with family, taking long, reflective walks, and having the courage to get out of the rat race. What would you say in an obit for a friend who has chosen to live the simple life? What would you say in an obit for yourself?

193

Some would say that the more we have, the more we are faced with fears about losing what we have. Would you agree or disagree with this? Why? How is this true or false in your personal life?

194

Thomas Merton once wrote, "Not all people are called to be hermits, but all need enough silence and solitude in their lives to hear the deep inner voice of their own true self at least occasionally." When do you hear your "deep inner voice"? What has your "deep inner voice" been trying to tell you lately?

195

When it comes to living a life
of simplicity, what cultural
influences will require the
greatest resistance on your part?
Why?

196

In some Asian countries,
one of the methods used to
capture monkeys is to take a
hollow gourd, bore a small hole
in it, place a piece of fruit inside,
then tie it to the ground. When
the monkey reaches inside for the
fruit, it is unable to get its
clenched fist free. Of course, if it
wanted to escape, all the monkey
would need to do is let go of the
fruit. But often it does not do so
and ends up becoming someone's
supper. What is something you
want so badly that your clinging
to it prevents you from
experiencing freedom
and simplicity?

197

How can the pursuit of wealth, rank, or reputation hinder one's relationships with others and complicate one's life? In what ways have you personally experienced this?

198

In what ways does loneliness drive people to lead hectic, cluttered lives? How has this been true in your life?

199

Albert Einstein once said, "Art is the expression of the profoundest thoughts in the simplest way." What is the most profound thought that you want your life to express? What is the simplest way to express it?

200

Sometimes, in order to go forward, we are required to go backward a few steps first. If you desire to move toward a life of simplicity, in what ways might you be required to first take a few steps back?

201

Short of selling everything and moving to a monastery or a cabin in the woods, what are three things you can begin doing now to move toward a simpler lifestyle?

Author

JERRY JONES is a free-lance writer working on his first historical novel. Over the past 20 years he has helped edit, write or develop more than 25 books, served as editor of three national periodicals, and helped launch a national ministry. He lives in a small cottage along a creek in the mountains near Colorado Springs, Colorado, and is trying to learn more about what it means to live a simpler life.

IMPROVE YOUR SMALL GROUP AND PERSONAL RELATIONSHIPS.

201 Great Questions

Ideal for getting conversations started in small groups or for hanging out with friends, this book gives you the opportunity to learn more about others--and about yourself.
201 Great Questions
(Jerry D. Jones) $6

201 Great Questions for Married Couples

Here's an in-depth resource to get beyond the surface to the topics that really matter. Whether you've been married five or fifty years, this creative communication tool will enhance your relationship. Useful for both individual and group reflections.
201 Great Questions for Married Couples
(Jerry D. Jones) $6

201 Great Questions for Parents and Children

This easy-to-use tool helps parents interact with their children to build mutual understanding and deeper family relationships as they discuss their perspectives and problems.
201 Great Questions for Parents and Children
(Jerry D. Jones) $6

How to Ask Great Questions

Questions can make or break your small group, Sunday school class, or meeting. Learn how to ask questions that build relationships, draw out opinions, guide people to solve a problem, and much more.
How to Ask Great Questions
(Karen Lee-Thorp) $6

Get your copies today at your local bookstore, visit our website at www.navpress.com, or call (800) 366-7788 and ask for offer #**2294** or a FREE catalog of NavPress products.

NAVPRESS ◐

BRINGING TRUTH TO LIFE
www.navpress.com
Prices subject to change.